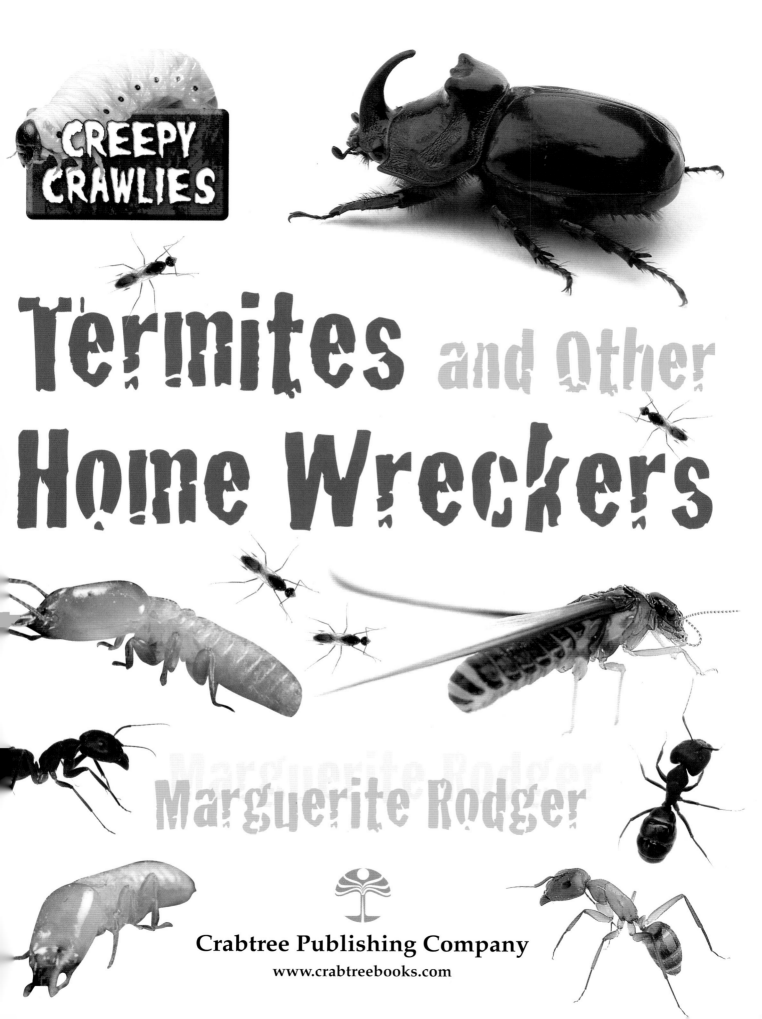

CREEPY CRAWLIES

Termites and Other Home Wreckers

Marguerite Rodger

Crabtree Publishing Company

www.crabtreebooks.com

Developed and produced by
Plan B Book Packagers

Author:
Marguerite Rodger

Editorial director:
Ellen Rodger

Art director:
Rosie Gowsell-Pattison

Logo design:
Margaret Amy Salter

Editor:
Molly Aloian

Proofreader:
Crystal Sikkens

Project manager:
Kathy Middleton

**Production coordinator
& prepress technician**:
Katherine Berti

Photographs:
Istockphoto: Atelopus: p. 16 (bottom); Silent Wolf: p. 27 (top)
Photos.com: cover, logo photograph
Shutterstock: cover, p. 1–2; 2happy: p. 8; akva: p. 27 (middle);
    Alslutsky: p. 11 (top left, top right, and bottom right);
    Alexey Avdeev: p. 21 (bottom); Evgeniy Ayupov: p. 3,
    5 (top), 15, 23; Steve Bower: p. 5 (bottom), 13 (bottom);
    Bonita R. Cheshier: p. 22 (top); Dionisvera: p. 7 (top);
    EuToch: p. 22 (bottom); Melinda Fawver: p. 4 (middle);
    Four Oaks: p. 9 (bottom); Karel Gallas: p. 29 (top);
    gmwnz: p. 26; Anton Harder: p. 12; Mark Herreid:
    p. 4 (bottom); Brendan Howard: p. 10 (top); Eric Isselée:
    p. 25 (bottom); Linda Johnsonbaugh: p. 28 (bottom);
    Greg Kieca: p. 20; Laila R: p. 25 (top); Henrik Larsson:
    p. 4 (top), 13 (top), 14; Doug Lemke: p. 26 (top); MarFot:
    p. 27 (bottom); Mikhail Melnikov: p. 11 (bottom left),
    29 (middle); Mr. Brightside: p. 9 (top); NatalieJean:
    p. 25 (middle); orionmystery@flickr: p. 24 (bottom left);
    Michael Pettigrew: p. 17; Dr. Morley Read: p. 16 (left);
    Fedor Selivanov: p. 24 (bottom right); Ssguy: p. 6 (top);
    Margaret M Stewart: p. 29 (bottom); Vinicius Tupinamba:
    p. 7 (bottom), 16 (top); p. Uzunova: p. 21 (top); Bonnie
    Watton: p. 6 (bottom); Liew Weng Keong: p. 10 (bottom);
    zonesix: p. 28 (top)

Library and Archives Canada Cataloguing in Publication

Rodger, Marguerite
    Termites and other home wreckers / Marguerite Rodger.

(Creepy crawlies)
Includes index.
ISBN 978-0-7787-2503-9 (bound).--ISBN 978-0-7787-2510-7 (pbk.)

    1. Termites--Juvenile literature. 2. Wood borers--Juvenile
literature. I. Title. II. Series: Creepy crawlies (St. Catharines, Ont)

QL529.R63 2010   j595.7'36   C2010-902037-5

Library of Congress Cataloging-in-Publication Data

Rodger, Marguerite.
    Termites and other home wreckers / Marguerite Rodger.
        p. cm. -- (Creepy crawlies)
    Includes index.
    ISBN 978-0-7787-2510-7 (pbk. : alk. paper) -- ISBN 978-0-7787-2503-9
(reinforced library binding : alk. paper)
    1. Termites--Juvenile literature. 2. Household pests--Juvenile literature.
I. Title. II. Series.

    QL529.R63 2011
    648'.7--dc22   2010011671

Crabtree Publishing Company
www.crabtreebooks.com   1-800-387-7650

Printed in China/072010/AP20100226

**Published in Canada
Crabtree Publishing**
616 Welland Ave.
St. Catharines, Ontario
L2M 5V6

**Published in the United States
Crabtree Publishing**
PMB 59051
350 Fifth Avenue, 59th Floor
New York, New York 10118

**Published in the United Kingdom
Crabtree Publishing**
Maritime House
Basin Road North, Hove
BN41 1WR

**Published in Australia
Crabtree Publishing**
386 Mt. Alexander Rd.
Ascot Vale (Melbourne)
VIC 3032

Contents

Wood borers and munchers are not very popular with humans.

Some home wreckers, such as these winged termites, are smaller than a dime.

What is smaller than a dime, but can eat through a house? A wood-boring insect! Termites, wood-boring beetles, and ants are small **pests** that are known to cause **havoc** on buildings by chewing through wood. While they may be small, the damage they cause is enormous.

Wood Munchers

Wood-boring insects are any insects that dig or chew holes into wood. Some of these insects are simply looking for shelter while others are looking for their next meal. Termites and wood-boring beetles eat the wood that they bore into, while ants dig into wood to find a cozy place to build their nests. These three are not scientifically related to one another, but they have a lot in common. Their day-to-day activities ruin homes and businesses.

The Bad News...

Just how much damage can these little pests cause? It is estimated that termites alone cause billions of dollars in damage each year in the United States. This is because they are speedy eaters. A small **colony** of 60,000 termites can eat through one foot (0.3 m) of wood in six months. Termites wreck more homes than hurricanes, floods, and earthquakes combined!

The Good News...

While it may seem like wood-boring insects cause more harm than good, it is important to remember that they are around for a reason. They only become pests when they **interfere** with human life. In nature, carpenter ants play an important role in maintaining forests. Carpenter ants make their nests in wood and eat wood–eating insects. Their constant chewing and digging creates tons of sawdust that rots. This decomposing sawdust is a great natural **compost**. Termites also do good in nature. Termite colonies eat wood, which they digest and turn into fertilizer for plants.

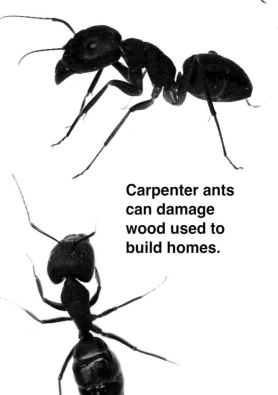

Carpenter ants can damage wood used to build homes.

CRAWLY FACT

Social Insects

Termites and ants are social insects. They are considered social for three reasons: mature insects take care of the young, the generations overlap, and they have castes, or social classes. The queens are at the top of the social insect caste. Their job is to reproduce. There are also worker insects, who spend their days building shelters, gathering and storing food, and taking care of the young. Termite colonies are also known to have specialized "soldiers" that protect the colony against invaders.

Wood-boring insects become pests when they show up at your home uninvited. They dig through your walls and construct "shelter tubes" out of their own poop, spit, and sawdust. They can damage homes beyond repair. Carpenter ants can build nests in your walls and refuse to leave.

They Are Many

Insect scientists, also called **entomologists**, have identified about 2,600 **species** of termites. They estimate that there might be closer to 4,000 varieties out there! Out of all these species, only about ten percent of them are true pests. This means that only a fraction of termites in the world cause actual damage to homes, forests, and crops. Termites are grouped according to what they eat. These groups include grass-eating, **subterranean**, soil-feeding, dry-wood, and damp-wood eaters. Out of these five groups, it is usually only the subterranean and the dry wood varieties of termites that cause damage to homes and buildings.

Worker termites feed the other members of the colony their digested food, either from the mouth or the anus!

Wood damaged by termites, ants, or beetles is fragile and crumbles easily under pressure.

They Bite Too?

There are over 600 species of wood-boring beetles, but fewer than ten of these species are considered house pests. These include the creepily-named deathwatch beetle and the common furniture beetle. There are over 1,000 species of ants. The most common ant pest in North America is the carpenter ant and there are over a dozen species of them. Some carpenter ants bite and can inject a painful acid into skin. Although their looks may drive you buggy, termites, wood-borer beetles, and carpenter ants do not carry or spread any diseases.

Rhinocerous beetles are named for the horns that males have. They are large beetles sometimes kept as pets in southeast Asia, but better known as pests because they kill coconut palm trees by eating the leaves.

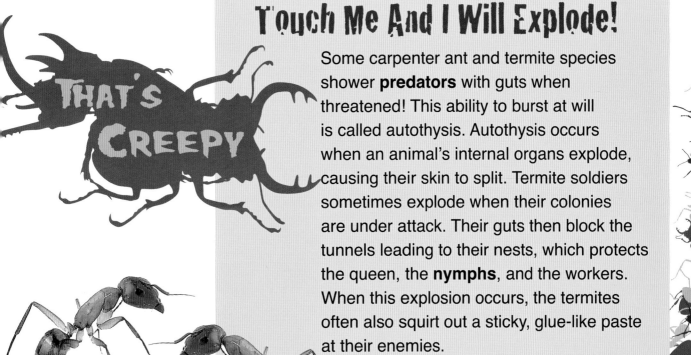

THAT'S CREEPY

Touch Me And I Will Explode!

Some carpenter ant and termite species shower **predators** with guts when threatened! This ability to burst at will is called autothysis. Autothysis occurs when an animal's internal organs explode, causing their skin to split. Termite soldiers sometimes explode when their colonies are under attack. Their guts then block the tunnels leading to their nests, which protects the queen, the **nymphs**, and the workers. When this explosion occurs, the termites often also squirt out a sticky, glue-like paste at their enemies.

Pest Story

Every pest has a story. Wood-boring insects have been around since the time of the dinosaurs. These insects have **evolved**, in order to adapt to new environments and survive in the changing world.

Stuck in Time

In 1998, **amber** containing prehistoric ants was found in New Jersey. It was estimated to be 92 million years old. They are the oldest known **fossil** ants. Scientists can learn a lot from fossils, including the ways in which insects have changed over time.

Evolution of a Poop Eater

Entomologists know that termites are related to cockroaches. They have some things in common, such as a special case that surrounds their head for protection. However, they are also very different, which is why it was such a shock to discover how closely related they are.

Termites eat wood, while cockroaches eat anything, including the poop of other cockroaches. Gross, but true! It is this fact that led entomologists to believe that termites may have even evolved from cockroaches. The theory is that when termite ancestors ate each other's poop, they were sharing important **microbes** that eventually allowed termites to digest wood!

Termites are often referred to as white ants, but they are in fact related to cockroaches.

Bug Worshipers

Beetles have fascinated humans for thousands of years because of their variety of colors, sizes, and crazy habits. In ancient Egypt, these insects were even **worshiped**. Over 4,000 years ago, the ancient Egyptians believed that the scarab beetle represented Khepri, the god of the rising Sun. The scarab beetle, also known as the dung beetle, rolls animal poop into large balls and then eats it. The beetle was worshiped because the way that it rolled the dung reminded the Egyptians of the way that Khepri was said to roll the Sun through the sky day after day. Egyptians carved stones and molded pottery into scarab beetle shapes. Wearing beetle jewelry or being buried with it was custom, as the jewels represented renewal, and it was hoped that they would ensure rebirth in the **afterlife**.

Carved or molded scarab beetle amulets and jewelry were made from pottery, stone, gold, and glass. They were usually inscribed with patterns or designs that represented royalty.

Dung beetles are skilled rollers of poop.

It may be hard to believe, but there are over 1,000 species of carpenter ants, and over 2,800 species of termites. There are 15,000 different species of metallic wood-boring beetles. When scientists find an insect, how do they figure out what type it is? How do they name the insect if it is a new species? Scientists sort and group insects using a system first developed nearly 300 years ago. Keeping track of all those insects is no small feat, as new ones are being discovered all the time!

A Class For All

All animals, including insects, are identified and named using a classification system developed by Carl Linnaeus, a Swedish scientist. In 1735, Linnaeus wrote a book called *Systema Naturae*. The book was only eleven pages long, but it described several different species of plants and animals. Linnaeus revised his book as new plants and animals were discovered. By 1767, the thirteenth copy of the book was 3,000 pages long!

Carl Linnaeus' classification system has changed since his time and is more scientifically accurate today.

Carpenter ants belong to a large family.

Kingdoms, Family, and Class

Linnaeus' system to help name and describe living things was called taxonomy. He divided the animals into kingdoms. Originally, Linnaeus named only three kingdoms, but scientists today use six, including Animalia, Plantae, Fungi, Protista, Archaea, and Bacteria. He broke kingdoms down into phyla, into which animals are placed based on their body structure. Then, each phylum was divided into even smaller groups according to class, family, genus, and finally, species. Over time, other scientists altered the classification system to make it more scientifically accurate. Living things are now divided according to kingdom, phylum, class, order, family, genus, and species. Today, everything is classified using common descent, instead of common features.

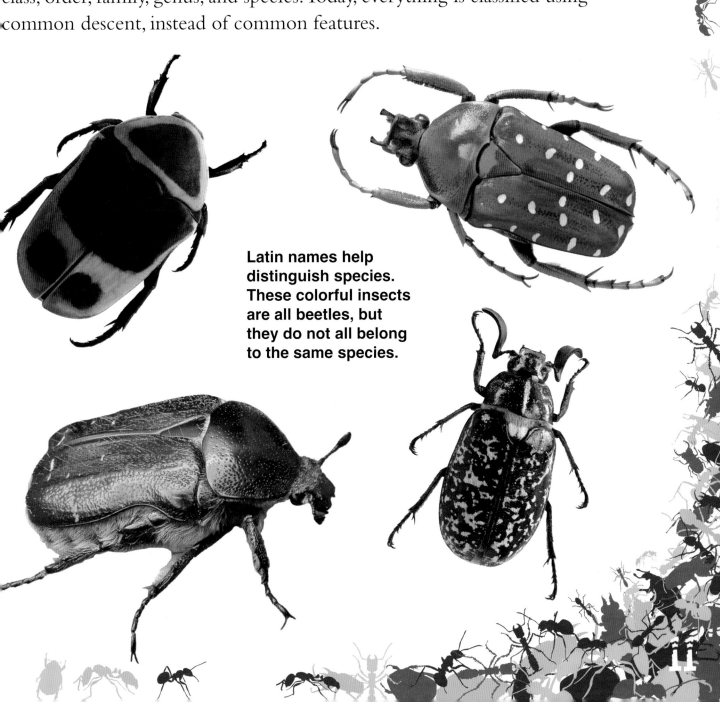

Latin names help distinguish species. These colorful insects are all beetles, but they do not all belong to the same species.

Isoptera

Termites belong to the phylum Arthropoda, the class Insecta, and the order Isoptera. All insects belong to the class Insecta. Termites belong to one of seven different termite families. While about 2,600 species of termites have been formally identified by scientists, they estimate that there are over 4,000 in total. All Isoptera have very soft bodies, and are almost always light in color. They also have mouths shaped for chewing. All termites species share these characteristics, but they can be different from one another in some ways, too. For example, some termite species live in nests or mounds, while others choose to make themselves at home in your house.

Only ten percent of the world's termites are pest species. Termite species in warm savanna regions build large mounds that can be 30 feet (9.1 m) high.

Coleoptera

Wood-boring beetles belong to the order Coleoptera. Coleoptera has more identified species in it than any other order in the entire animal kingdom! The order of Coleoptera got its name because it means "shield wing," which is a great way of describing the hard wings. Many families within the Coleoptera order contain different species of wood-boring beetles. Many wood-boring beetles have interesting common names that help describe them. Some examples include old-house borers and the flat-headed wood borer. Scientists estimate that 20 percent of all species on Earth are beetles.

A metallic wood-boring beetle closeup

Hymenoptera

Carpenter ants belong to the order known as Hymenoptera. The Hymenoptera order also includes other insects with thick or heavy wings, such as bees and wasps. The black carpenter ant belongs to the Formicidae family, and the genus Camponotus. Black carpenter ants can range in size from one-quarter inch to three-quarters of an inch long. All sizes can live together in the same colony. They like to live either outdoors or indoors, in damp or decaying wood. When the wood is wet or rotting, it is much easier for the ants to dig into to hollow out a home for themselves!

Carpenter ants are named for their ability to build nests in wood.

Anatomy Lesson

What makes an insect an insect? How does a newly discovered insect earn its rank in the Insecta class? The answer is in the structure of its body! All insects have common features. These body features set insects apart from other animals, and help them to find food and shelter while defending themselves from potential dangers.

BEETLE BODIES

Beetles have elytra, a set of protective, leathery wings.

The beetle's hemolymph, or blood, protects it from freezing in cold temperatures.

Some beetles have an iridescent, multi-colored surface. The color is caused by many stacked, dish-like layers that make up the outside of the bug. These small layers are slanted, and point in different directions, reflecting the light around the beetle, like a prism.

Pincer-like mandibles on the beetle's head help them chew food. Beetles use their antennae to smell and feel the environment around them.

Ant Bodies

Carpenter ants may not be brightly colored, but they do have their own fascinating quirks. They are usually black, or reddish brown, and sometimes they have wings. Their antennae are bent and are used to detect vibrations and feel for potential obstacles. Ants have three small ocelli (eyes) on the tops of their heads to help them see whether it is light or dark.

ANT ANATOMY

Simple eyes, called ocelli, are sensitive to light but do not show visual images. Also attached to the head are two feelers that help ants communicate.

Ants have three main body parts: a head, a thorax, and an abdomen. Ants have exoskeletons, or skeletons on the outside of their bodies.

The poison sac is located on the metasoma.

Mandibles, used for chewing, are located on the head.

Ants have six legs attached to their thorax. At the end of each leg is a claw. Ants do not have lungs but breathe through tiny holes in their bodies.

Termites with Wings

Each termite in a colony has a special job. Reproductive termites are known as the queens and kings. Their wings are incredibly thin and delicate. Termites are terrible flyers, so once they find an acceptable place to reproduce and lay eggs, they usually shed their delicate wings. The queen's already large body is able to stretch to lay up to 2,000 eggs a day. When the queen is this large, she needs the help of the worker termites to get around.

Termite colonies have different castes. Each caste has a different role. There are workers, soldiers, reproductives (queens and kings), and supplementary reproductives. The supplementary reproductives take over if a king or queen dies.

KING

A king is thinner than the queen.

QUEEN

The queen termite is very large.

Workers and Soldiers

Worker termites are yellow or whitish in color. Their job is to feed other termites. The food consists of partially digested wood. In order to feed the others, the worker termites have special **organisms** in their gut that help them to digest the wood they eat. After they have digested the wood, they feed it to the others. Soldier termites work hard to defend their colony. They use their large heads and jaws to block the narrow tunnels that lead to their nests, in order to keep predators out. Soldiers have poor vision, but they are great at biting intruders, and they can even shoot poisonous glue from their nasi (nose).

SOLDIER

The soldier termite has mandibles that stick out from its head that are used to protect the colony.

Termites have three sets of legs attached to their thorax.

A termite's three main body parts are its head, thorax, and abdomen. Its antennae and eyes are located on its head.

Life Cycles

Beetle Life Cycle

There are four stages in a beetle's life cycle: egg, larva, pupa, and adult. Some species of wood-boring beetles complete the transition from egg to adult in a matter of months. Some beetles remain in the larval stage for up to 30 years!

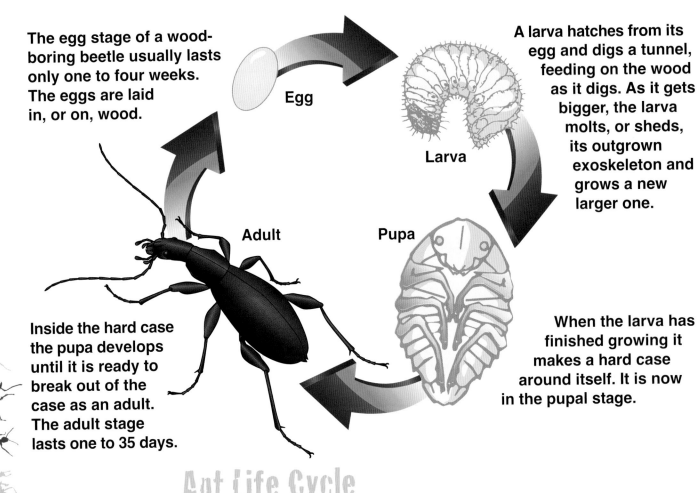

The egg stage of a wood-boring beetle usually lasts only one to four weeks. The eggs are laid in, or on, wood.

Egg

A larva hatches from its egg and digs a tunnel, feeding on the wood as it digs. As it gets bigger, the larva molts, or sheds, its outgrown exoskeleton and grows a new larger one.

Larva

Adult

Pupa

Inside the hard case the pupa develops until it is ready to break out of the case as an adult. The adult stage lasts one to 35 days.

When the larva has finished growing it makes a hard case around itself. It is now in the pupal stage.

Ant Life Cycle

To reproduce, male carpenter ants and new queens laid by the colony's queen leave their colonies to mate in a swarm. Once carpenter ants have mated, the male dies. The new queens fly off to start new colonies. Queens lay eggs for about 15 days! They stay with the eggs until they start to hatch and feed the young from their salivary glands. It takes 60 days to go from eggs to adults.

Ant life cycle

It takes about 60 days for a carpenter ant to develop from egg to adult. Larvae hatch from the eggs in about 24 days. They grow and develop for about 20 days. The pupal stage is about 21 days long.

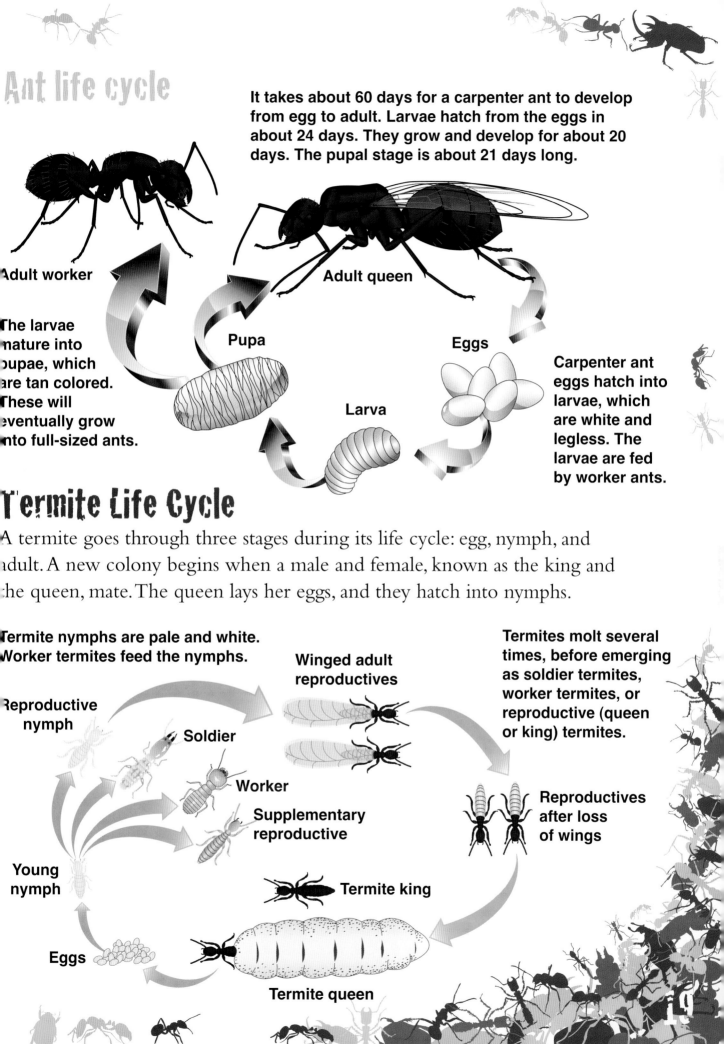

Adult worker

The larvae mature into pupae, which are tan colored. These will eventually grow into full-sized ants.

Adult queen

Pupa

Eggs

Larva

Carpenter ant eggs hatch into larvae, which are white and legless. The larvae are fed by worker ants.

Termite Life Cycle

A termite goes through three stages during its life cycle: egg, nymph, and adult. A new colony begins when a male and female, known as the king and the queen, mate. The queen lays her eggs, and they hatch into nymphs.

Termite nymphs are pale and white. Worker termites feed the nymphs.

Winged adult reproductives

Termites molt several times, before emerging as soldier termites, worker termites, or reproductive (queen or king) termites.

Reproductive nymph

Soldier

Worker

Supplementary reproductive

Reproductives after loss of wings

Young nymph

Termite king

Eggs

Termite queen

All wood-boring insects choose the location of their homes for very specific reasons: food and a place to reproduce safely.

Live Where You Eat

Termites live where they eat. Many pest species of termites invade human-made structures because the wood is ideal for eating. These termites are called dry-wood termites. Dry-wood termites do not need water to survive. They can live off the cellulose, or plant fiber, that they eat, and the moisture within it. They can live deep inside your walls, attic, or eaves. They may also eat telephone poles, dead trees, and furniture.

This tree could have a sign that says: termites ate here.

Opportunity Knocks

Ants live where there is a good chance that they will find moisture, or water. This is why they make their homes in moist or decaying wood. Their parent colony, or original colony, is outdoors, in rotting trees or stumps. Satellite colonies, or colonies formed by ants who have left the parent colony, are found indoors, near sources of water such as leaks. Porches, decks, and even windowsills are **vulnerable** to carpenter ants. The ants find a crevice or a crack and begin to chew their tunnels into the wood. They do not eat the wood that they chew, and sawdust can often be found near the entry hole. Ants know that they need easy access to food, so they sometimes build their nests near kitchens in order to be near sweet treats, such as soda or fruit!

You can sometimes follow ants back to their nests.

Tunneling In

Wood-boring beetles live in furniture, hardwood floors, trees, and even books! They will live anywhere they can dig a tunnel. There are many different types of borer beetles. Some destroy wood, but others prefer to ruin crops! Two of these insects, the coffee berry borer and the white stem borer, are small but mighty. These beetles are known to be the most harmful pests to coffee crops and can be found in more than 70 countries. Other notable beetle pests are the grain and flour beetles. These pests can be found in bags of flour, boxes of cereal, spice jars, and pancake mixes.

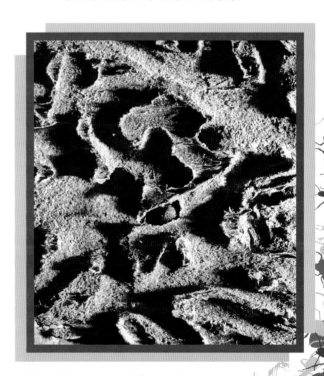

Beetles tunnel in and destroy trees and wood.

Infestation!

Wood-boring insects may be small, but they sure can cause a fuss! They can cause a lot of damage, and once they are detected, it can take a whole team of people to get rid of them.

They're Heeeeere!

When a building is infested, it is overrun with pests. Wood-boring beetles infest homes in order to lay their eggs. Termites move in when they are looking for food and warmth. Carpenter ants are simply looking for shelter. Each of these pests may have a different reason for barging in, but the results are always irritating.

Home Inspection

Many experts agree that the best way to find a pest is through a home inspection. Inspectors, look in and around homes to find evidence of pests. These professionals search everything from crawlspaces to basements to attics, looking for damaged wood, mud tunnels, sawdust, and even the insects themselves.

Termites love the warm, wet climate of Hawaii. They infest up to 15 percent of homes in the state.

The subterranean tube or above ground mud tunnel is a sure sign that termites have moved into a building.

Extermination

What happens if the inspector finds a pest invasion in your home? Sometimes, the solution is simple: create a barrier so that the pests cannot enter your home! For example, some experts install a wire mesh around the house so that the insects cannot access the home. **Exterminators** are often hired to deal with pest problems. They use **pesticides** and baits to kill pests. Once the insects eat the poisoned wood, they crawl back to their colonies, where the poison slowly kills the whole colony. Although pesticides may be a quick fix, there are some definite downsides! Poisons can be very dangerous—especially for pets and small children! Also, insects have a history of adapting to **resist** pesticides. This means that they evolve or change in order to survive the poisoning!

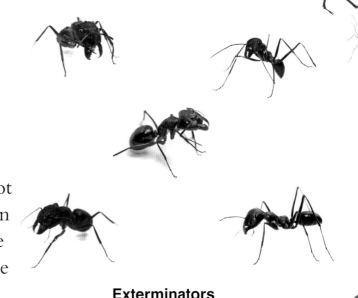

Exterminators may use wood injected with poison to tempt the insects!

CRAWLY FACT

Friendlier Pest Control

Using poison to control infestations is not the only option. Natural substances, such as boric acid, have been known to kill insects! Boric acid is a white powder that is found in some deserts, such as the Mojave Desert in California. When boric acid is eaten by insects such as termites and ants, the bugs slowly dry out and die. Sometimes, sugar is added to the boric acid to make the mixture more appealing to ants. The good news for us is that boric acid is harmless to humans.

While many people work very hard to get rid of wood-boring pests, some people search them out for different reasons. Some people consider wood-boring insects a delicious and **nutritious** treat! In Indonesia and Africa, termites are fried or roasted for humans to eat as a snack! Many animals feed on these insects, too.

Snakes and Birds

Many different types of snakes eat termites. Birds also love to eat insects. The woodpecker is a perfect example of a bird that loves to eat wood-boring insects. Small lizards, such as the gecko and the skink like to snack on termites, too. However, the biggest predator of the termite is the smallest of them all: the ant. The ant and the termite are **mortal** enemies! Despite their best efforts, sometimes the soldier termites cannot keep the ants away.

Geckos and ants are termite eaters.

Welcome to the buffet, anteater! Anthills and termite mounds represent a tasty meal for predators.

Bears and Anteaters

Many mammals love the taste of a termite treat. These predators usually have natural advantages: long tongues and muzzles, curved claws, and an excellent sense of smell. The sloth bear, a bear found in India and Nepal, falls into this category. The sloth bear loves both termites and ants, and its specialized nostrils can close quickly once the bear has inhaled its prey. Anteaters live in Central and South America. They love to eat termites and ants, using their long tongues and claws to capture them! One species of anteater, called the giant anteater, eats up to 30,000 insects a day! Aardvarks, native to Africa, are also termite eaters.

Fire ants will eat other ant species. Anteaters, Aardvarks, and armadillos also eat ants.

Creepy Lore

Wood-boring insects have both frustrated and fascinated people for centuries. They have also proven inspirational, influencing everything from literature to compact car designs.

KEEPING WATCH

Deathwatch beetles can really creep people out. These wood eaters often live in the rafters of old, creaky buildings, where they make tapping or ticking sounds on silent summer nights. Their eerie noises are meant to attract potential mates. They are called deathwatch beetles because it is said that they keep the dying company when they are bedridden. Some people even believe that hearing or seeing a deathwatch beetle is a sign that someone is about to die! Many famous authors have taken advantage of this beetle's bad reputation. Edgar Allen Poe, a famous poet, wrote about the creepy critter in his poem "The Telltale Heart." A murderer in the story hears the deathwatch beetle tapping while he keeps watch over his victim.

DIDGERIDOOS

Cave paintings in Australia that are over 20,000 years old depict the first instrument ever made by termites. Yes, by termites! Termites played a huge role in the making of a traditional **Aborigine** wind instrument called the didgeridoo. Before modern manufacturing, Australian Aborigines made didgeridoos from eucalyptus tree branches hollowed out by termites. Aborigine didgeridoo makers could tell which trees had hollowed limbs. A branch was then cut to the right length, and a mouthpiece added.

DRIVE A BEETLE

The Volkswagen Beetle was first produced in 1938, in Germany as an economy car. First called the *Käfer*, the German name for beetle, the compact, round car reminded people of the insect. It is also nicknamed "bug." The Beetle holds the record for the longest produced same-model car.

YOU CAN'T SIT STILL?

Have you ever had ants in your pants? This common expression is used to describe someone who just cannot sit still. Ants crawling in your pants would feel itchy and creepy and would make you jerk and shake.

THE BEATLES

Of all the British rock groups that have come and gone, the most successful one also has a link to a creepy crawly: the beetle! The band spelled its name with an "ea" instead of a double "e" as it brought the musical term "beat" to mind. The buggy name is a tribute to Buddy Holly and the Crickets, another band.

Myth and Fact

Termites, beetles, and ants are cool insects. They have survived for millions of years, but we are still learning more about them. Here are some little known facts and common myths about these creepy crawlies:

Some people think they are safe from termites because they live in brick homes in northern areas. Not true! Termites are found all over North America, except in the far north. Most homes have wooden frames that termites can easily reach by tunneling through cracks in concrete or brick.

Carpenter ants have a sweet tooth! In your home they are drawn to sugar, syrups, and jams. That's why you'll often find them in the kitchen.

Termite nests can be huge! The largest termite mounds ever recorded were found in Australia and Africa. The Australian mound was 20 feet (6 m) wide. The African mound was 42 feet (13 m) high.

This termite nest is almost as high as an elephant's eye.

Many species of beetle larvae live in dirt. The larvae, called grubs, are the origin of the word "grubby." To be grubby is to be dirty.

Beetle-wing art is an ancient Asian art form where the wings of metallic wood-boring beetles were used to decorate pictures, clothing, and textiles. The beetle wings made the art shiny and vibrant. Today, beetle-wing art has mostly died out, but tourists can sometimes find beetle-wing earrings and other jewelry in Thailand, India, and China.

Pest Detective

Wood-boring pests are cool to learn about, but creepy to encounter in your own kitchen! To learn more, check out these fantastic Web sites, books, and museums:

Here are some cool sites to check out:

WEB SITES

Pestworld for Kids
www.pestworldforkids.org
This is a great site for learning about insects of all kinds. Find pictures, read infosheets, get homework help, and play games. You can also learn fun science experiments that you can do at home.

Bug Bios
www.insects.org
This Web site provides information on all sorts of insects for budding bug enthusiasts. The entolinks section has links to entomological societies, university entomology departments, and other sources of insect information.

Smithsonian Institution: BugInfo
www.si.edu/Encyclopedia_SI/nmnh/buginfo/start.htm
Look up different types of bugs and insects, and research special topics such as insect flight, and pheromones. A list of science fair projects help you learn more and have fun.

Bio Kids
www.biokids.umich.edu/critters/Insecta
Learn about the habitats and habits of termites, beetles, and other insects with this easy to understand site that answers all your questions.

KidInfo: Insects
www.kidinfo.com/Science/insects.html
This site is a great place to start research. It provides links and descriptions of other useful sites on insects, as well as photos and videos.

Here are some great books on termites, ants, beetles, and other insects:

Termites: Hardworking Insect Families,
by Sandra Markle. Lerner Publishing, 2009.

The World of Insects Series
Crabtree Publishing, 2005/2006.

Ants and Termites by Anna Claybourne.
Black Rabbit Books, 2004.

Want to see termites, beetles,
and ants up close and personal?
Here are some great places to visit:

American Museum of Natural History
Central Park West at 79th Street
New York, NY 10024-5192
Phone: (212) 769-5100

The Insect Zoo at San Francisco Zoo
1 Zoo Road
San Francisco, CA 94132
Phone: (415) 753-7080

Invertebrate Exhibit, The National Zoo
3001 Connecticut Ave., NW
Washington, DC 20008
Phone: (540) 635-6500

The O. Orkin Insect Zoo at the National
Museum of Natural History, Smithsonian
10th Street and Constitution Ave., NW
Washington, DC 20560
Phone: (202) 633-1000

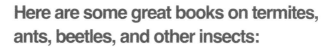

Glossary

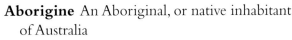

Aborigine An Aboriginal, or native inhabitant of Australia

amber The fossilized resin of a prehistoric tree that sometimes contains the remains of insects

afterlife A life after death

colony A community of insects living together

compost Decaying or rotting organic matter, such as plant matter, that is used as a plant fertilizer

entomologist A scientist who studies insects

evolved To have developed certain traits over several generations

exterminator A person that gets rid of, or kills, pests

fossil The remains of a prehistoric living thing preserved in rock or the fossilized resin amber

havoc Widespread destruction

interfere To prevent something from being carried out or finished

microbe A microorganism or bacterium that causes disease

mortal Liable to cause death

nutritious A food that nourishes or is necessary for growth and good health

nymphs Larvae, or immature stage of growth

organisms Plants, animals, or other life-forms

pests Destructive insects or animals that attack crops, food, homes, or livestock

pesticide A substance used to kill pests, harmful insects, and animals

predators Animals that prey on others

resist To withstand something or the effect of something

species A group of living things that have similar characteristics and are capable of interbreeding

subterranean Existing or living under the Earth's surface

vulnerable Susceptible or liable to attack

worshiped Adored or honored as a god

Index